Transformed
into the Image of Jesus

A Discipleship Workbook to Help You Grow as a Christian

Richard B. Ramsay

Transformed Into the Image of Jesus
A Discipleship Workbook to Help You Grow as a Christian

Richard B. Ramsay

© copyright by Richard B. Ramsay, 2025
ISBN: **979-8-90046-942-3**
Staten House

Previous edition published as *Pressing On*
© copyright by Richard B. Ramsay, 2012
Independently published in Lulu.com, 2012

Published in Spanish as *A Su Imagen*
Published in 2000 by Editorial UNILIT

Bible quotations are from the *New International Version* (NIV84), as taken from Logos Software, unless Indicated otherwise.

And we all, with unveiled face,
beholding the glory of the Lord,
are being transformed into the same image
from one degree of glory to another.
For this comes from the Lord who is the Spirit.
(2 Corinthians 3:18, ESV)

...I press on to take hold of that for which
Christ Jesus took hold of me.
(Philippians 3:12, NIV84)

The Author

Dr. Ramsay was a missionary in Chile for 21 years, teaching in a seminary and planting churches. There he met his wife, Angelica. They now live in Florida and they have two adult children. For the past 25 years, they have worked internationally in distance education, traveling to teach classes and producing resources for theological education and leadership training. Richard has taught for *Universidad FLET* and *Thirdmill Seminary* and has developed many online courses.

He holds a D.Min. degree and an M.Div. from *Westminster Theological Seminary*, as well as a Th.M. from *Covenant Theological Seminary*.

Other books by the author include *The Certainty of the Faith, Am I Good Enough?, Basic Greek and Exegesis, Intellectual Integrity, Catholics and Protestants, Strengthen Your Faith, Synopsis of the Bible, Putting the Pieces Together,* and *Orientation for Leaders.*

CONTENTS

Dedication

To Angélica, who more than anybody else on earth has
encouraged me to become more like Christ.

Thanks

I would like to thank Sue Yarbrough and Erika O'Shee for many of the drawings used in this booklet. Erika did the line drawings and Sue did some of the other graphics.

I would also like to thank the people who have encouraged me and given me feedback on the lessons over many years. They were first written in Spanish (called *A Su Imagen*), and most of the feedback has come from friends in Chile and Cuba. It is gratifying to hear how these lessons have helped people grow in their spiritual walk. There is an amazing revival occurring in Cuba, and over 20,000 of these booklets, as well as the same number of *Am I Good Enough?* (called *¿Cuán Bueno Debo Ser?* in Spanish) have been printed and used in home cell groups throughout the island.

Preface

Just a closer walk with Thee
Grant it Jesus, is my plea
Daily walking close to Thee
Let it be, dear Lord, let it be.

(Hymn by unknown author)

Would you like to be more like Jesus? Would you like to have a closer walk with Him? The purpose of this workbook is to help Christians grow, using the tools that God has given us, while trusting God for the results. The Holy Spirit "transforms" us into the image of Christ (2 Corinthians 3:18), yet we also "press on" to receive what He Himself provides for us (Philippians 3:12). In this discipleship manual, you will study biblical guidelines for things like prayer, studying the Scriptures, having a Quiet Time, sharing your faith, discovering your spiritual gifts, teaching a Bible Study, and finding God's will for your life. It will help you become more like Jesus and encourage you to keep your eyes on Him, the "author and perfecter of our faith," as you "run the race" (Hebrews 12:1-2).

One of the greatest sources of confusion among Christians today is related to the process of spiritual growth and the work of the Holy Spirit. During the history of the Church there have been periods when important doctrines have been defined, like the Trinity, the canon of the Bible, and justification by faith. Many of the current debates are producing a better understanding of sanctification, the topic of this book.

Some people emphasize human responsibility, and others emphasize the sovereign work of God for Christian growth. This book tries to harmonize the two. Even though all fruit of spiritual growth comes from the Lord, and even though salvation is by faith from beginning to end, man also has a responsibility to use the means of grace given to him. Faith and obedience are inseparable.

You can write out the answers to the questions in the spaces provided.

We encourage you to study this booklet in a group, so that you can share and encourage each other.

May the Lord bless you abundantly as you study His Word and put it into practice!

PART 1

YOU ARE A NEW PERSON

INTRODUCTION

If you sincerely trust in Jesus Christ as your Lord and Savior, you have been born again and have a new identity.

READ JOHN 3:3-6.

What must happen before a person can enter the kingdom of God? What do you think this means?

When you were born again, the Lord gave you a new heart and you began to trust in Him. Your sins were forgiven and you turned your life over to Him. This was *the beginning of a new life.*

READ 2 CORINTHIANS 5:17.

How does this verse describe the believer?

This doesn't mean that every aspect of your person has been changed. You still have the same physical appearance, for example. (When the Lord returns, you will also have a new body, but not yet!) Nevertheless, there has been a spiritual change so significant that the Bible describes you as a *new person.* In the following lessons, we are going to study the characteristics of this change.

1. YOUR NEW POWER

When you put your faith in Jesus, you gained access to His power over sin in your life. You have a center for decision-making in your heart, and when you were born again, your self-centered *ego* stepped down from the throne and the Lord took over. He is the new king. Jesus directs your life and gives you power to overcome sin.

READ ROMANS 6:14.

What change has occurred in the life of the Christian with regard to sin?

Sin no longer dominates the believer, because the Holy Spirit is in his heart. "But sometimes it still seems like sin overcomes me," you say.

READ ROMANS 7:15-25.

Can you identify with this struggle that Paul describes? How would you explain this struggle in your own words?

What is Paul's only hope for victory in this struggle? (vs. 25)

In other words, we should be realistic and admit that we still struggle with sin. Its power still lingers within us. This does not mean that we can excuse our wrong-doing by saying, "I can't help it!", or "The devil made me do it!" The influence of sin is still there, but now we can choose to resist it, and the Lord gives us strength to overcome it. God's grace is always available to us.

Neither are we *spiritual schizophrenics*. That is, we don't have two *personalities* that are battling against each other. Sin is still alive, but it is not a part of our new identity. It no longer *belongs* in us. It is a foreign enemy.

The history of humanity is a spiritual war, in which the victory was declared when Jesus rose from the grave. Yet enemy soldiers are still hiding in the shadows of their demolished headquarters taking shots at us. The same thing happened in your heart when you let Jesus come in and rule. You have a new spiritual government, but the enemy still attacks. The good news is that our new leader will not let us be destroyed.

This whole book is about how to win the victory in this struggle.

READ EPHESIANS 4:22-32.

How does Paul describe the process of spiritual transformation in this passage?

Again, we see from this text that, while in one sense you are already a new person, in another sense you are going through a long *process* of *putting on* your new nature. This means to abandon sin and develop a wholesome new life.

Mention the things that you should put aside:

We can't simply stop doing *bad* things; we have to replace them with *good* things.

I knew a young man who had a fervent desire to be good. He decided not to take a bus to work because it always went faster than the speed limit and he felt guilty about it. Then he refused to go to work because another person in his office listened to music that he considered a bad influence. Little by little, he isolated himself from the world to the point of closing himself up in his house. He didn't want to go out into the street because this meant confronting too much temptation. Even though he was thirty years old, he stayed home with his mother who took care of him. Obviously, this is not the lifestyle that God wants us to live! To do nothing is also to sin, because there are many good things left undone. How can we love people if we are sitting at home alone, completely out of touch with them?

Mention the good things we should put on in place of the bad things, according to Ephesians 4:22-32.

In some people the Lord makes dramatic changes right away. For example, there are cases of drug addicts and alcoholics who have been freed from their dependence instantly. However, this is not what happens in most Christians. Normally, the changes are gradual. Spiritually, we are like children who grow up, gradually leaving behind self-centered habits, learning to love others. The big difference is that the

Holy Spirit lives in our heart and gives us strength to live this new life. Sin is still there, but it is no longer *in control*.

READ JOHN 15:4-5.

What must we do to bear fruit? How would you explain this analogy in your own words?

To *remain* in Jesus means to *trust* in Him. Just as a plant receives its nourishment through the roots, we obtain spiritual strength from the Lord.

Sometimes when you read passages such as Ephesians 4:22-32, you may think, "Do I have to change all this? I can't be like that!" However, this way of thinking reveals two problems:

1. In the first place, you are looking too much at yourself, instead of God. What we want to show in these lessons is that you are a new person guided by the Spirit of God, and *HE* will help you change. Of course, you have your own responsibility in this process of growth (and we will study that in other lessons), but the power to change comes from the Lord.

2. Secondly, you may not be appreciating how *encouraging* these changes are. They are not a *burden*. Instead, it is a great *relief* to be able to become more like the person

Ephesians 4 describes. You will experience greater peace and joy. The Lord *frees* us from sin.

Now read the following passage in another way. Don't think of what a *heavy burden* you have as a Christian. Read the passage as a *promise*. Think of it this way: "How wonderful that the Lord will do this in me!"

READ COLOSSIANS 3:5-17.

Write down the negative things the Lord will take out of you:

Note the positive things that the Lord will produce in you:

FOR PERSONAL REFLECTION:

1. Reviewing the two lists of sins that we should overcome (Ephesians 4:22-32 and Colossians 3:5-17), which ones cause you special difficulty?

2. Reviewing the two lists of positive things that the Lord will produce in us (Ephesians 4:22-32 and Colossians 3:5-17), which are the characteristics that you especially desire and need?

REVIEW

Explain what it means that you are a *new person* in Christ.

NOTE: You can look at the answers to the review questions at the back of the book to confirm your answers.

FOR GROUP DISCUSSION:

1. Mention some of the positive changes you have seen in your life since you became a Christian.

2. What if it still seems that some sin has power over you? Does that mean that you have not been born again? What can you learn from Romans 7:15-25 to help you with this?

3. What would you say to the young man who stayed in his house to avoid temptation?

2. YOUR NEW PURPOSE

FOR PREVIOUS REFLECTION:

Can you define the fundamental purpose of your life? What is it? Why?

INTRODUCTION

A long time ago people thought that the earth was the center of the universe and that the sun revolved around it.

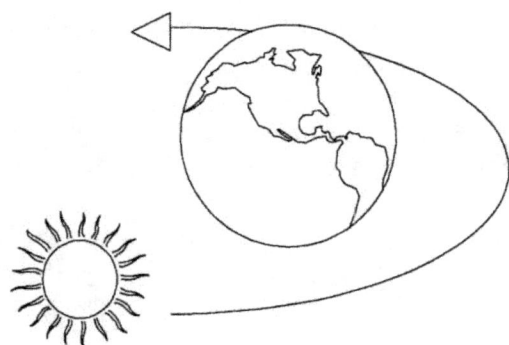

Then they realized they were wrong; the earth revolves around the sun!

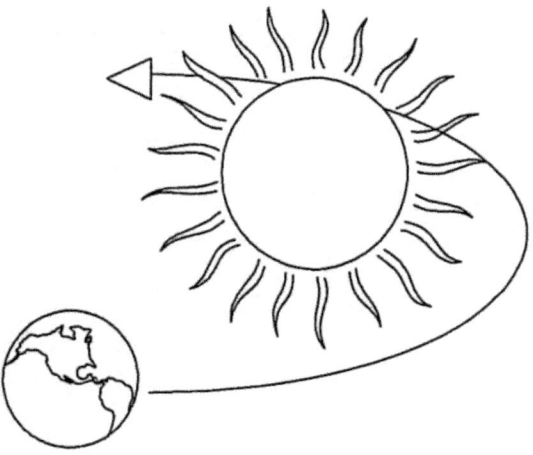

This is the way it is with our lives: Before we are born again as Christians, we try to be the center of our own lives. Then when we believe in Jesus, we leave our sins at the cross and turn our lives over to Him. He becomes our center. We commit ourselves to be His disciples and to do whatever He asks us.

Hebrews 12:2 says, "Let us fix our eyes on Jesus, the author and perfecter of our faith."

To advance in the Christian life, we need to know where we are going. What is the purpose of our life and the goal of our growth?

THE PURPOSE OF LIFE

Look up the following verses to see what our purpose in life should be:

       1 PETER 4:11

       1 CORINTHIANS 6:20

       ROMANS 15:6

What is your conclusion?

This purpose can be expressed in different ways. For example, Jesus summed up what God expects of us in the following verses:

READ MATTHEW 22:36-40.

Express it in your own words:

Paul says it another way:

READ ROMANS 14:8.

How would you say this in your own words?

The *Westminster Shorter Catechism*, question #1, says:

> "What is the chief end of man?"

> Answer: "Man's chief end is to glorify God and to enjoy Him forever."

THE GOAL OF GROWTH IN CHRIST

READ ROMANS 8:29.

For what purpose were we predestined?

READ EPHESIANS 4:11-13.

What is the task of the leaders of the Church?

What does this tell us about the goal of our spiritual growth?

To summarize:

> The *purpose* of your new life is to
> GLORIFY GOD,
>
> and the *goal* of your growth is to
> BECOME MORE LIKE JESUS.

READ PHILIPPIANS 3:8-12.

Where does Paul's righteousness come from? (v. 9)

How does he obtain it?

This does not mean that we are passive in the process of spiritual growth. In a somewhat mysterious way, God enables us to participate. Paul says, "I press on to take hold of that for which Christ Jesus took hold of me." (NIV84)

The purpose of this book is to help you *press on* toward your goal of being like Christ, while trusting Him completely for the results.

THE TWO BROTHERS

There is an evangelistic tract called "The Two Brothers." It tells about a murderer who is sentenced to death. His brother, who was a very good person, loved him so much that he dressed in his clothes and went to die in his place. He left his own clothes with a note for the one who had been condemned to die, that said, "My dear brother, I took your place today. I only ask one thing of you, that you put on my clothes and live the kind of life I was living."

That is what Jesus has done for us: He died in our place, so that could be free from condemnation, and so that we could begin a new life. Now he asks us to put on His character and live our lives the way He would.

What is Jesus like? Since we know He was perfect, we will look at two passages that tell us about perfect righteousness: one gives a list of the *Fruit of the Spirit*, and the other describes *Love*.

A. THE FRUIT OF THE SPIRIT

READ GALATIANS 5:22-23.

List the characteristics of the Fruit of the Spirit:

B. LOVE

READ 1 CORINTHIANS 13:4-7.

Write the characteristics of love:

READ JOHN 20:21.

What does this verse tell you about the purpose of your life?

Your "job description" is to continue the kind of life that Jesus Himself lived. Think of it! You are very important! You are like an *angel* sent from God to help needy people and share His Word with them. Of course, you can't die to save people from their sin as Jesus did, but you can continue the ministry of Jesus in the sense that you serve God by loving the people around you.

You can't do this on your own. You must depend on the Holy Spirit to give you strength, and you also depend on the help of other Christians.

Neither can you fully reach the goal in this life. You will not be perfected until the Lord returns and transforms us into His image. In the meantime, you will be growing, just like a child grows into an adult.

REVIEW

1. Your new purpose in life is:

2. The goal of your spiritual growth is:

3. Jesus manifests the F _____ of the S _____.

4. Jesus manifests perfect L _____.

5. What is your "job description" as a Christian?

FOR DISCUSSION

1. What seems to be the purpose of life for people you know who have not committed their lives to Christ?

2. Explain how your work (or your studies) can glorify God. (Don't think just about how you can talk to others about Christ, but about how your job *itself* makes some contribution to society.) What would happen if you didn't do it? For example, if you work at a typewriter all day, how does this work glorify God? What role does it have in the organization you work for, and how does the organization benefit society? If you are a mechanic, why should you do a good job of fixing cars? What would happen if you didn't? Try to analyze your work in this way and see if you can appreciate the dignity of your day-to-day activities. Everything you do is for the glory of God.

PART 2

TAKE A LOOK IN THE MIRROR

INTRODUCTION

The first step toward growth is to take an honest look at ourselves. If we try to hide our weaknesses, we will never overcome them. We have no reason to pretend that we are okay when we are not, since we know that God loves us despite our sin and wants to help us overcome our problems. In Christ, we are free to be authentic. The object of the next two lessons is to help you to *take a look in the mirror*, according to God's Word, to see where you need to change. We'll study the Ten Commandments for this purpose.

READ JAMES 1:22-24.

What point is James making here?

READ 1 JOHN 1:8-10.

According to John, why should we admit we are sinners?

READ ROMANS 12:3.

According to Paul, how should we think about ourselves?

3. FOUR WAYS TO LOVE GOD

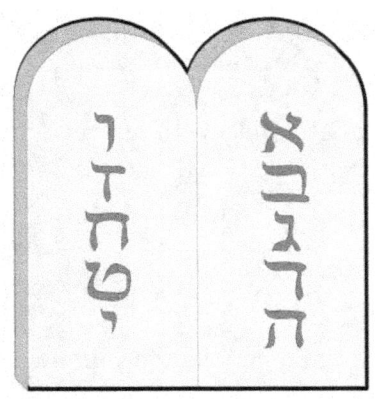

Sometimes we may think of the Ten Commandments as negative limitations. However, the Lord gave them to us partly for our own benefit. If we live according to His norms, we will live a more satisfying and joyful life. We should obey His commandments *primarily* because it pleases *God*, but this in turn will also give *us* joy. The two aspects are inseparable. As the catechism question says, our main purpose is "to glorify God *and* to enjoy Him forever" (*Westminster Shorter Catechism*, Question 1).

When a child gives his father a hug, he wants to show his affection, but the gesture also gives him a sense of joy and comfort. In a similar way, when we please God, we also receive benefits.

God wrote these commandments with His own finger on tablets of stone, so we know they are important. They summarize some key elements of what He expects of us, and they reflect His own character.

Most people are somewhat familiar with the commandments but have never really analyzed carefully what they mean. Let's take a fresh new look at them!

The first four deal especially with our relationship with God. They show us how to love Him.

READ EXODUS 20:1-17.

#1. Write the first commandment in your own words (20:3):

This first commandment is fundamental, because it tells us who God is and that He is the only one we should honor.

Can you think of different ways in which we sometimes break this commandment?

In general, any person, any ideology, any ambition, or any possession, which becomes more important than God Himself, is another *god* to us, and we have broken the first commandment.

#2. Write the second commandment in your own words. (Exodus 20:4-6).

Can you think of ways in which we sometimes break this commandment?

Why is this so important to God? Partly because anything man can make is a poor representation of God. His glory is beyond our comprehension. Would you like your friends and family to keep a picture of you that made you look ugly, or which somehow misrepresented you? How would you feel if they kept a statue of a cow to remember you?! That's the way God feels when we use statues or other physical objects to remind us of Him or help us worship Him.

READ 1 TIMOTHY 2:5.

According to this verse, who is the only mediator between God and man?

#3. Write the third commandment in your own words (Exodus 20:7).

37

Can you think of ways in which we sometimes break this commandment?

This commandment includes much more than what we consider *dirty language* or *swearing*. It forbids doing anything that dishonors God or gives Him a *bad name*. That may mean *speaking* about God or *thinking thoughts* about God that don't honor Him. It could also mean committing some sin that reflects poorly on God. In general, it includes anything that takes glory away from God.

#4. Write the fourth commandment in your own words. (Exodus 20:8).

There are two sides to this:

We should _____ during six days, and _____ on the seventh day.

Sometimes we can be lazy, and this commandment reminds us that we are supposed to work. On the other hand, and it seems to be more and more common today, many people are turning into *workaholics*. They don't know how to stop. They have no time for their families, and they don't have time to go to church. However, man is made with a need to rest, to restore himself both physically and spiritually. If he tries to work incessantly without sufficient sleep and without time off, he will eventually break down like machinery that is not properly maintained. Notice that we should also let others rest on the seventh day.

It's interesting to note that after Jesus' resurrection, the disciples changed the day of rest from Saturday to Sunday. They began to worship on the first day of the week instead of the seventh, to celebrate the day of His resurrection. However, some people still insist that Saturday should be considered the day of rest.

READ ROMANS 14:5-10.

What does this passage teach regarding which day we should observe as a day of rest?

The important thing is that time should be set aside to renew both our physical and our spiritual strength.

REVIEW

Write a phrase to sum up each of the first four commandments:

1.

2.

3.

4.

FOR DISCUSSION:

1. Have any of the first four commandments taken on new meaning for you? Which ones? What have you learned?

2. Is there something you still don't understand about any of them?

3. As you *look in the mirror* and examine yourself according to these four commandments, in what areas do you need to change?

FOR PRAYER:

Ask the Lord to help you grow in the areas where you have found weaknesses.

4. SIX WAYS TO LOVE YOUR NEIGHBOR

While the first four commandments deal especially with man's relationship with God, the last six deal especially with man's relationship with other people. Keep in mind, however, that these two aspects are inseparable. That is, if you love God, you will love your neighbor, and if you love your neighbor, you are also loving God.

Furthermore, just as we explained that by loving and obeying God, we also receive benefits and joy, the same principle applies to loving others. When we love others, we are also blessed in return. All three dimensions are inseparable: God, others, and ourselves.

READ MATTHEW 22:36-40.

How does Jesus summarize the law? What are the two main precepts?

It is important to recognize that the commandments talk about *relationships*, both with God and with man. Jesus does not sum up the law by saying simply, "be good," as if we could become righteous in some abstract sense. Rather He tells us to love God and to love others as ourselves. Love is not simply an emotion; love means treating each other the way God says we should.

Notice also that loving ourselves is part of the formula. Jesus is not condoning self-centeredness, but rather a wholesome regard for our own well-being. Despising ourselves, or disregarding ourselves, does not help us love others; on the contrary, it only makes it more difficult.

READ EXODUS 20:12-17.

#5. Write the fifth commandment in your own words (20:12):

There is a principle of respect for authority here which should be applied not only to the family, but also to other structures of society. Without submission to authority, everything would be in chaos.

42

Can you mention other ways in which this commandment should be obeyed?

#6. Name the sixth commandment (Exodus 20:13):

READ MATTHEW 5:21,22.
_____

In what other ways do we sometimes break this commandment?

#7. What is the seventh commandment? (Exodus 20:14)

READ MATTHEW 5:27-30.
_____

In what ways do we sometimes violate the seventh commandment?

#8. Name the eighth commandment (Exodus 20:15):

Can you think of different ways in which we might sometimes steal?

#9. Write the ninth commandment in your own words (Exodus 20:16):

Mention ways in which we might sometimes be dishonest:

READ JOHN 8:44.

Where do lies originate?

#10. What is the tenth commandment? (Exodus 20:17)

Covetousness is an unwholesome desire for something that does not belong to you. Not all desires are wrong, of course. There's nothing wrong with wanting to read a good book, or to eat a good meal, under normal circumstances. Sexual desires are perfectly normal within marriage. On the other hand, some desires are inappropriate: for example, to desire another man's wife, to want a car that is priced beyond your financial means, or to have an unsatiable appetite for chocolate.

Can you think of things that you sometimes *covet*?

REVIEW

Write all ten commandments in your own words, using a phrase for each one:

1.

2.

3.

4.

5.

6.

7.

8.

9.

10.

FOR DISCUSSION:

1. Has your understanding of the last six commandments changed? In what way?

2. Are there any questions that you have about any of them?

3. With which ones do you struggle most?

FOR PRAYER

Ask the Lord to help you grow in your weak areas.

PART 3

HOW CAN I CHANGE?

INTRODUCTION

After looking in the mirror, we realize that we need to change. We are far from being what God expects of us. But *how* do we change? You can't simply decide to be a better person. How many times have you been frustrated by attempts to overcome your weaknesses and problems? You need more than good intentions. You need an internal strength that only comes from the Holy Spirit.

READ ROMANS 1:17.

From whom does righteousness come?

What do we need to obtain it?

Notice that this righteousness that comes from God is by faith *from first to last*. Our lives are like a bridge that is held up by strong pillars of the grace of God on both ends, and we walk over it by faith, from beginning to end.

READ GALATIANS 3:3.

What was Paul's concern about the Galatians?

5. THE TOOLS TO GROW

READ HEBREWS 12:1-2.

To what is life compared here?

What should we do as we run?

Why? What does Jesus do for our faith?

Never take your eyes off Jesus! If you do, you will fall, just like a runner who begins to look around at the other athletes, to watch someone in the stands, or to stare at his own feet. To keep your eyes on Jesus is the secret for spiritual growth.

READ 2 CORINTHIANS 3:16-18.

Into what are we transformed when we look at Jesus?

We are like a child who imitates his father. Since he loves him and is constantly around him, he becomes very much like him. Again, the secret is to keep your attention on Jesus.

But we are not passive in this process of growth. God has given us tools. We call them the *Means of Grace* because they are the means that the Lord uses to communicate His grace to us. Our strength comes from Him, and precisely because of that fact, we should use the tools that He has given us. What are these tools?

Look up the following passages and try to discover the *Means of Grace* mentioned in each one:

2 TIMOTHY 3:16-17

EPHESIANS 6:18

1 CORINTHIANS 11:23-26

ACTS 8:36-38

ACTS 2:42

HEBREWS 10:25.

We will study how to use these four *Means of Grace* in the following lessons:

> The Bible
> Prayer
> The Sacraments
> Fellowship

REVIEW

1. What is the secret for significant change in your life?

2. Our righteousness comes from God, by F_____ from first to last.

3. Name the four *Means of Grace* mentioned in this lesson.

FOR DISCUSSION:

1. Which of the *Means of Grace* do you think you have used most? Which have you used least?

2. What do you think happens to a person who is not trusting the Lord to grow, but trying to change himself by his own strength? How can you detect this problem?

FOR PRAYER

Ask the Lord to teach you how to use the *Means of Grace* to become more like Him. Ask Him to help you be willing to make the necessary changes in your lifestyle to make full use of these tools for growth.

6. HOW TO STUDY THE BIBLE ON YOUR OWN

In the next few lessons, we will look at the *Means of Grace*, one at a time. We'll start with the Word. One of the most significant things you can learn as a Christian is to study the Bible on your own. You can discover profound truths to believe, promises to claim, principles by which to live, and comfort in troubled times. You will no longer have to depend only on the ideas and teachings of other people; you can also study on your own.

READ ACTS 17:11.

Why were the Bereans considered *more noble*?

READ JOHN 8:31-32.

According to this passage, why should we study the Word of God?

READ 2 PETER 1:19-21.

Why is the Bible a special book?

READ 2 TIMOTHY 3:16-17.

For what things is the Bible useful?

In this lesson, we will teach you a simple method of personal Bible study. It will help you analyze a short passage. Read the following steps carefully, then do the exercise to practice them:

THREE STEPS OF BIBLE ANALYSIS

I. OBSERVATION (What does the passage say?)

II. INTERPRETATION (What does it mean?)

      A. Ask yourself questions.
      B. Look for the answers.
          1. In the Bible itself
          2. In other study aids

III. APPLICATION (What importance does it have for me?)

      A. Promises
      B. Truths
      C. Ethical principles
      D. Examples

Now memorize these steps:
What are the three main steps?

      O _____

      I _____

      A _____

Which of the three steps:

a. ...looks for the details of the passage?

b. ...looks for the meaning of the passage?

c. ...looks for the importance of the passage in your life?

What are the two subdivisions of *Interpretation*?

      A. _____

      B. _____

What are the two sources for finding answers?

      1. _____

      2. _____

Note the four possible kinds of application:

      A. _____

      B. _____

      C. _____

      D. _____

EXERCISE

Practice the steps of Bible Analysis with John 3:16. It's a well-known verse, but you will be amazed at how many new things you discover!

First, pray that the Lord will guide you and teach you new things.

I. OBSERVATION

After reading it carefully, write the verse *in your own words*:

II. INTERPRETATION

A. Write down questions you have about the verse. This is important as you begin your analysis, because these questions will guide the rest of your study.

Suggestions:
> What does "world" mean in this verse?
> What does it mean to "believe" in Jesus?
> What is "eternal life?"

B. Look for answers to your questions:

Depending on the question, you may do some of the following procedures:

1. Read the passages surrounding this verse.
2. If your Bible has notes with references to other passages, you might look them up to see if they help understand the verse you are studying.
3. If you have one, use a concordance, which shows a list of the Bible passages where a word is used. For example, you might see how "world" is used in other passages to gain a better understanding of possible meanings in the verse you are studying.
4. If you have one, you can look up words or concepts in a Bible Dictionary.
5. You might see what theologians say in commentaries, or in the notes your Bible may have. Talk with your pastor to see what books he recommends.
6. You might want to install Bible software to have access to Bible dictionaries and commentaries. We recommend e-Sword, for example. It is free and offers lots of resources. (See https://www.e-sword.net/)

Write down the answers you are finding:

III. APPLICATION

After meditating on the needs in your own life, in your family, in your church, and in the rest of society, look for one or more of the following:

  A. A promise
  B. A truth
  C. An ethical principle
  D. An example to follow

Write down applications. Hopefully, there are several. Make them concrete and specific, not vague and general. Think of how the passage should change your thinking, your actions, and your feelings ("head, hands, and heart").

Good! You probably found much more in this verse than you had anticipated. Now, take a moment to pray. Ask the Lord to help you put into practice what you have learned.

REVIEW

Write the steps for Bible analysis:

I.

II.

        A.

        B.

                1.

                2.

III.

        A.

        B.

        C.

        D.

FOR DISCUSSION:

1. Share what you discovered in your study of John 3:16.

2. Share what you learned about Bible analysis.

7. HOW TO PRAY MORE EFFECTIVELY

Prayer is simply talking to God. It can include the following elements:

Praise
Thanksgiving
Confession of sin
Requests

READ MATTHEW 6:5-15.

In verses 5-7, Jesus mentions two problems that the hypocrites have regarding prayer.

What are they?

According to verse 8, why is it not necessary to use many words?

Notice that the Lord's Prayer is totally centered on God. For example, we should pray that *His* name be "hallowed" (or "glorified"), that *His* kingdom come, that *His* will be done.

Analyze the prayer, writing down your understanding of each phrase:

a. "Our Father in heaven,"

b. "hallowed be your name,"

c. "your kingdom come,"

d. "your will be done, on earth as it is in heaven."

e. "Give us this day our daily bread."

f. "Forgive us our debts as we also have forgiven our debtors."

g. "And lead us not into temptation, but deliver us from the evil one."

According to verses 14 and 15, what happens if we don't forgive others who sin against us?

This could mean that when someone has so much bitterness in his heart that he simply can't forgive others, it shows that he has never understood God's forgiveness, that he has never accepted His forgiveness in Christ. However, it may also refer to something that can happen even to believers. When a Christian refuses to forgive someone, this puts a barrier between himself and God, temporarily impeding the benefits of forgiveness that he normally experiences in his daily walk with Christ. This fellowship will be restored when he comes to the point of forgiving the person who has offended him.

READ JOHN 14:13-14.

In whose name should we pray?

To pray *in the name of Jesus* does not mean simply to use a phrase, "In Jesus' name, amen," at the end of our prayer, as if this phrase were *magic* (although there is certainly nothing wrong with saying this phrase at the end of the prayer if we mean it sincerely.) Rather, it means to pray with the *attitude* of seeking His honor and submitting to His authority. It means that the motive of our prayer is to see that *His* will be done. To ask something *in Jesus' name* is to ask something *for Him* and *with His authorization*.

READ 1 JOHN 5:14.

How can we be sure we are asking something "according to His will?" Where do we find His will written down for us?

If we find that our request agrees with what the Scripture teaches, then we know that we are praying *in Jesus' name* and that God the Father will answer.

READ HEBREWS 10:19-22.

In the Old Testament, the *Most Holy Place* was the inner chamber of the temple, beyond the *Holy Place*. Only the high priest could enter this chamber after ceremonial cleansing and sacrifices. When Jesus died on the cross, the curtain between the *Holy Place* and the *Most Holy Place* was torn (see Matthew 27:51), symbolizing the fact that anyone who has been cleansed of his sin can now enter directly into the presence of God. This is what we do when we pray.

Why can we pray with confidence?

The Lord does not grant our petitions because we deserve it, but only because of Jesus. We are forgiven and washed with His blood, so we can enter the presence of God at any moment, in any place, with a clear conscience. We need no other mediator; we can talk directly with Him.

READ 2 CORINTHIANS 12:7-10.

What problem did Paul have?

NOTE: Most commentators think this was some kind of physical problem, possibly a problem with his eyes.

How many times did Paul ask the Lord to take away this "thorn in the flesh?"

What was the Lord's answer?

What does this teach us about prayer?

Sometimes He does not grant our request because it would not be the best thing for us. On the other hand, it may not be the right time yet.

READ MATTHEW 26:39-42.

What did Jesus pray?

What phrase did He add after his petition both times?

We should always pray with this attitude, that the Lord's will be done. Trust Him to do what is best!

REVIEW

1. What does it mean to ask something *in Jesus' name*?

2. How can we be sure we are praying *in Jesus' name*?

3. Why does the Lord sometimes *not* grant our requests?

FOR DISCUSSION

Have you learned something new about prayer? What?

IMPORTANT EXERCISE

Prepare a request for your prayer time, using biblical passages as a basis.

First, write what you would like to ask:

Now look up passages that support this petition.

Are there any promises? Write them down.

Can you think of any of God's characteristics that give you confidence that He will grant your request?

Try to think of any other biblical truths, some historical example, or anything that gives you reason to think that the Lord will want to do what you are asking:

Now you can pray with a solid basis and really trust the Lord to answer! You know that you are praying *in the name of Jesus!*

It is possible that, as you studied to prepare this prayer request, you realized that you were going to ask something that was not in accord with God's will or with biblical truths. In that case, it's a good thing you found out! You learned something important!

Also, be careful not to try to *manipulate* God. He is free to grant our requests or *not*. We may easily be confused about what we think is best, but He will never make a mistake; He will always work things out for our good (Romans 8:28). He is also free to choose the *timing* He considers best and the *way* He considers best. This exercise is to learn to make our prayers more biblical, more effective, and more God-centered. Nevertheless, God is not our assistant or helper that we can ask to do whatever we please. He is the owner of the universe, and He can do what He wants!

ANOTHER EXERCISE

If you would like to analyze other prayers in the Bible to see how requests are presented, you can look at the following passages:

Genesis 18:16-33

Numbers 14:1-19

Psalm 25

Philippians 1:3-11

Colossians 1:3-14

8. THE MEANING OF THE SACRAMENTS

The sacraments are ceremonies instituted by Jesus to teach the spiritual truths of the gospel by means of visible and tangible material symbols. Protestants celebrate only two sacraments, Baptism and the Lord's Supper, which replace circumcision and the Passover of the Old Testament.

I. CIRCUMCISION

READ GENESIS 17:10-14.

To circumcise means to cut the foreskin of the male sexual organ.

Who had to be circumcised? (verse 10)

At what age?

This ritual was a sign of what? (verse 11)

In the Bible, *covenants* were agreements between God and His people. Since God is the sovereign king, and since the two parties are not equal in power, biblical covenants take the form of authoritative promises and demands. In this case, God promised Abraham several things: a: a *place*; Palestine, b. a *people*; a great number of descendants that would later form the nation of Israel, c. *power*; their country was going to be strong, and d. His *presence*; God was going to be with them (see also Genesis 12:1-3). To receive these blessings, God demanded faith and obedience. To circumcise someone meant that they belonged to God's family, that they promised to trust Him and obey Him, and that they claimed the benefits of the covenant. When parents had their children circumcised, they were expressing their promise to do God's will in raising their children and their trust that God would also bestow on them the blessings of the covenant.

II. THE PASSOVER

READ EXODUS 12:1-14.

The word *Passover* comes literally from the verb meaning to *pass over* and has its origin in the events related to the Exodus from Egypt. In order to force Pharaoh to let His people go, God sent ten plagues. The last one was the death of all the first-born children. But the Lord wanted to save the Hebrews from this plague, so He gave them the instructions for the *Passover*.

What did they have to kill? (verse 3)

What did they do with the blood? (verse 7)

What did they do with the meat? (verse 8)

What happened where there was blood on the door? (verses 12 and 13)

73

Israel was supposed to celebrate the Passover every year. The ceremony reminded them of how death had *passed over* them, and how the Lord had saved their children.

III. BAPTISM

READ MATTHEW 28:18-20.

According to this passage, what ceremony should be performed on Jesus' disciples?

NOTE: This also includes women. While in the Old Testament, only the men could be circumcised, as representatives of their families, now women also receive the sign of the covenant.

READ ROMANS 6:1-4.

According to these verses, what does baptism symbolize?

READ GALATIANS 3:27.

What does baptism symbolize, according to this passage?

SUMMARY OF THE MEANING OF BAPTISM

Baptism does not guarantee the salvation of the person baptized, as if it were a magical ceremony. It is a symbolic representation of the gospel, using a public ceremony to act out the benefits of salvation and the promises of the covenant: cleansing from sin, new life in Christ, and receiving the Holy Spirit. The special emphasis of this sacrament is on being received publicly into the Christian family. When you are baptized, it indicates that you have been included in God's people, with all the benefits of the covenant, just as circumcision did in the Old Testament.

IV. THE LORD'S SUPPER

READ MATTHEW 26:26-29.

What does the bread represent?

What does the wine represent?

READ 1 CORINTHIANS 11:23-34.

What should each one do before participating? (verse 28)

What should each one recognize as he partakes? (verse 29)

SUMMARY OF THE MEANING OF THE LORD'S SUPPER

The Lord's Supper symbolizes many aspects of salvation at the same time: Christ's death for our sins, the unity of all believers, our dependence on the Lord, and the future banquet we will celebrate with Him. The special emphasis of this sacrament is to remember Jesus' death for us.

The Roman Catholic Church teaches that the bread and the wine actually are transformed into the body and blood of Jesus, as they are consumed. Protestants believe that they are symbols, but that they are very special symbols. They were chosen by the Lord Himself to communicate spiritual truths.

It's like the Bible. The Bible contains *words*, which are only symbols. However, the words were chosen in a special way by God so that they communicate His thoughts. Thus, they are not just any words, but *divine* words. In a similar way, God chose the symbols of the sacraments to communicate His promises. The sacraments teach us the truths of the gospel with tangible and visible symbols.

We say that the sacraments are *signs and seals* of the covenant of grace because they *symbolize* the promises of salvation and because they have the *official seal* (like the wax seal of a king on his letter in the Middle Ages) of God Himself. The Holy Spirit is present during the sacraments to make them effective.

REVIEW

1. What is a *sacrament*?

2. What does baptism symbolize? (Mention the special emphasis.)

3. What ceremony of the Old Testament is replaced by baptism?

4. What does The Lord's Supper symbolize? (Mention the special emphasis.)

5. What ceremony in the Old Testament is replaced by the Lord's Supper?

FOR DISCUSSION:

1. Did you learn something new about the sacraments in this lesson? Explain what you learned.

2. Do you have any questions about the sacraments? Explain your questions.

9. THE JOY OF FELLOWSHIP

An important aspect of our spiritual growth is developing friendships and sharing with other Christians. The church can be a place to feel at home, a place where you have a spiritual family. We call this having "fellowship." This is the fourth *means of grace*. We benefit more from the other means of grace when we *share* them.

READ PSALM 133.

Describe the result of fellowship among those who share the same faith. Can you think of a more modern way of expressing this?

READ JOHN 13: _____

What is the mark of a Christian? What shows people that we are disciples of Christ?

The love between Christians is a living picture of the gospel. The Fall brought conflict, but salvation brings reconciliation and unity.

READ HEBREWS 10:24-25.

While fellowship is joyful, we don't meet together only to have fun. According to these verses, in what ways can we help one another when we meet together?

READ PROVERBS 12:25.

What can make a person glad when he has a heavy heart?

Many people are very lonely and discouraged. It can lift our spirits to meet with other Christians, and we can also help others that need a kind word or a hug. It's also important to learn to listen compassionately to people who are suffering and not judge them or be "preachy" with them.

READ 2 CORINTHIANS 1:3-4.

What kind of experiences help us comfort others?

READ 1 CORINTHIANS 12:12-21.

What figure is used to describe the church in this passage?

What does this figure teach us about why we need each other?

READ ACTS 2:46-47.

What were some of the results when Christians met together during the time of the New Testament?

REVIEW

1. What is the fourth *means of grace*?

2. What characteristic is evidence that we are disciples of Christ?

3. According to Hebrews 10:25, we should stir up one another to...

_____ and _____,

not neglecting to meet together, but

_____ one another.

4. What figure is used to describe the church in 1 Corinthians 12:12-21?

FOR DISCUSSION:

1. In what ways do you participate in fellowship with other Christians? In what other ways could you seek fellowship?

2. Share an experience when Christian fellowship was encouraging to you. What made it helpful for you?

10. HOW TO HAVE A QUIET TIME

As the deer pants for streams of water, so my soul pants for you, O God. My soul thirsts for God, for the living God. When can I go and meet with God? (Psalm 42:1-2)

The fact that two people are with each other during the whole day does not necessarily mean that they are communicating well. Sometimes you have to lay aside your normal activities to have a quiet talk. It's the same in our relationship with the Lord. He is always with us, but we need to set aside some time to give Him our special attention. We need to develop the habit of seeking God, dedicating time to dialogue with Him. In this lesson you will learn how to have a *Quiet Time*. Study the steps in order to practice them afterwards.

THE PLACE

Find a private place where there will be no interruptions or distractions, where you sense the presence of God. Use the same place regularly, if possible.

A QUIET TIME CONSISTS BASICALLY OF TWO ASPECTS:

1. READING THE BIBLE
2. PRAYING AND MEDITATING

1. READ a paragraph or a chapter of the Bible, observing the details carefully. It's best to follow through a whole book of the Bible. For example, you may want to start in the *Gospel According to Matthew* and continue through the whole New Testament.

Take time to relax and think about the things you have observed in the passage. Ask yourself what the Lord is telling you today. It's better to read a short passage carefully than to read a lot without really understanding it.

For some people it is helpful to write down in a notebook things are learning and keep a *spiritual journal,* but everyone is different.

2. PRAY AND MEDITATE about the things the Lord has been teaching you. If you are keeping a journal, you might write down your prayer requests and motives for giving thanks.

Note: You may want to follow the three steps of *Bible Analysis* that you learned previously. However, you may not have time to do all these steps carefully every day. You may also want to study the same passage over and over for several days. Again, everyone has their own way, your preferences might also change from time to time. Remember the steps for a more careful analysis:

A. OBSERVATION
	Read carefully, noticing the details.

B. INVESTIGATION
	1. Ask yourself questions about the passage.
	2. Look for the answers in the same chapter, in other parts of the Bible, or in Bible commentaries.

C. APPLICATION
	1. A promise,
	2. A new truth,
	3. An ethical principle, or
	4. An example.

Try to make this exercise a habit. For most people, it's best to have a *Quiet Time* daily, but don't feel guilty if you develop another habit that works better for you. You will soon realize that it is one of the most important decisions that you have ever made. The Lord will change your life as you study His Word and pray.

...But his delight is in the law of the Lord [the Scriptures] and on his law he meditates day and night. He is like a tree planted by streams of water which yields its fruit in season and whose leaf does not wither... (Psalm 1:2-3)

REVIEW

Write the steps for a *Quiet Time*:

FOR PERSONAL REFLECTION:

1. Do you already have a habit of a *Quiet Time*?

2. If not, would you like to start one?

FOR DISCUSSION

Do you have any other suggestions for a good *Quiet Time*?

IMPORTANT EXERCISE

Practice the steps for a *Quiet Time* with some passage in the Bible. You might start with the *Gospel of John*, studying the first paragraph.

PART 4

HOW CAN I HELP OTHERS GROW?

INTRODUCTION

In previous lessons we studied several aspects of personal growth. The goal is to be like Jesus. To grow closer to Him, we use the *Means of Grace*: The Word, prayer, the sacraments, and fellowship with other believers.

However, true growth also prepares us to help *others* grow. Our sanctification is not only filling our own individual *spiritual tank*, but also learning to minister to others. Every believer is a *minister*, in that sense. In the following lessons, we will study different aspects of the ministry. We want to become like Jesus, not only in His character, but also in His ministry.

READ MATTHEW 28:18-20.

These verses have been called the "Great Commission." What does this mandate include?

What gives us confidence that our efforts to fulfill it will be effective?

READ 2 TIMOTHY 2:2

What does Paul ask Timothy to do?

Notice that this means *four generations* of teaching. Jesus taught Paul, Paul taught Timothy, Timothy teaches others, and these in turn teach still others! This is how it should be! It's a process of multiplication.

11. THE MINISTRY OF EVERY BELIEVER

READ JOHN 20:21.

According to this verse, why are we sent into the world?

As mentioned in a previous chapter, we are to continue the work of Jesus. Of course, we can't die for the sins of other people, but we can love them in many ways, just like Jesus.

Let's look at the different elements of Jesus' ministry:

Look up the following passages and note which aspects are mentioned:

MATTHEW 9:35

What three things did Jesus do?

MATTHEW 11:25

MARK 1:35

MATTHEW 26:20

We could summarize the ministry of Jesus in the following six terms:

> 1. WORSHIP (He praised God the Father.)
> 2. PRAYER
> 3. TEACHING
> 4. SERVICE (He healed the sick.)
> 5. EVANGELISM (He "preached the good news.")
> 6. FELLOWSHIP (He spent time with the disciples.)

It's interesting to see that the disciples also did the same six things:

Write the phrase or the verse reference that suggests the corresponding ministry:

a. Prayer

b. Worship

c. Teaching

d. Service (helping the needy)

e. Evangelism

f. Fellowship (being together)

The following drawing of a cross illustrates these six aspects of the ministry, symbolizing the fact that Jesus dwells in us and carries out His ministry through us.

THE MINISTRY

1. Worship
2. Prayer

7. Fellowship

6. Service

5. Evangelism

3. Teaching
4. Sacraments

The arrows indicate the objects of the respective ministries. Worship and prayer are at the head of the cross, looking up to *God*. Teaching and the sacraments are at the base, aimed at strengthening and building up *the church*, giving it a firm foundation. Service and evangelism are the arms that extend into *the world*. Service also ministers to the *church*. In the middle, we get together to have fellowship, cooperating in these tasks and encouraging one another.

If any aspect of the ministry of a believer is missing, it is incomplete. The ministry of every believer should be *integral*. Just like whole grain bread is healthier because it has all the vitamins, an *integral* ministry is healthier, too.

REVIEW

Make the drawing of the cross with the six elements of an integral ministry.

QUESTIONS FOR DISCUSSION

1. Which aspects of the ministry are stronger in your own life?

2. Which are weaker?

3. Which ones are stronger in your local church?

4. Which ones are weaker?

5. What can you do to have a more integral ministry in your life?

6. What can you do to have a more integral ministry in your church?

12. WHY SHOULD I GO TO CHURCH?

In the following lessons we are going to study the six aspects of the ministry of the church and of every believer. We will begin with worship.

We go to church to receive the blessings of the preaching and the sacraments, as well as to share with other believers. However, there is an even more important reason to go to church: TO WORSHIP GOD.

When we think of the *ministry*, we usually think only of how we can minister to other people, but in a sense, our worship is a way of ministering to God. He does not *need* our ministry in the same way people do, but He *enjoys* our worship.

READ JOHN 4:23-24.

What does this teach us about worship?

To worship *in spirit* means to worship with your heart, sincerely, not just with your mouth. To worship *in truth* means to worship with your mind, using true concepts, not just with emotion.

On the one hand, it is not sufficient to sing a hymn with good words if you don't feel it in your heart. On the other hand, it's not right to sing a hymn with all your heart if the words are not biblical. Our praise should be both sincere and based on the Word of God.

READ EXODUS 5:1.

God told Pharaoh to let His people go so that they could do *what* in the desert?

After the Israelites were delivered from Egypt, they celebrated by *praising and worshipping* God. Then God gave them the law on Mount Sinai and told them to build a tabernacle where they would *worship* Him. (The tabernacle was a portable tent where the Lord manifested His presence.) Salvation leads to worship.

READ MATTHEW 2:2.

Why were the wise men looking for the baby Jesus?

READ REVELATION 4:11.

Why is the Lord worthy of praise?

READ REVELATION 15:4.

Why do the nations worship the Lord?

READ REVELATION 19:1-2.

What are other reasons to worship the Lord, according to these verses?

From beginning to end, the Bible tells us that man should worship God because of who He is and what He has done.

The word *worship* comes from a Greek word that literally means to fall down and kiss the feet of someone. This shows the attitude of worship. To prostrate before someone shows honor and submission. To kiss his feet shows gratitude. When we meet in a worship service, we are saying to the Lord, "We love you and honor you!"

Praise does not have to be *singing*, necessarily. We can praise God in prayer, too. It basically means expressing to God how wonderful He is.

Worship can be public or private, too. The worship service on Sundays is the most important activity of the *week* because it is the time when we meet with other members of God's family to worship Him. In the same way, our Quiet Time is the most important activity of the *day*.

We should clarify three points:

1. First, our whole life should be an act of worship in the sense that it should bring honor to God.

2. Secondly, if we are living a sinful life, even our acts of worship don't please God. (See Isaiah 1:1-20.)

3. Thirdly, even though our private individual worship pleases the Lord, it can't replace the Sunday worship service, where the whole church is united. All parents know how special it is to have all the members of the family sitting at the table. In a similar way, God is especially pleased by the public worship service.

REVIEW

1. What is the most important reason to go to church?

2. What does it mean, literally, to *worship*?

3. What does it mean to worship *in spirit and in truth*?

FOR DISCUSSION

1. What priority do you think *praise* should have in the worship service? Do you sometimes sense that the first part of the service seems like simply preparation to hear the sermon? How should we think of it?

2. What should our criteria be for selecting songs to sing in the worship service?

EXERCISE

Go somewhere to be alone with the Lord and dedicate fifteen or twenty minutes to do nothing but praise Him. Open your Bible to Psalm 103 (or some other passage if you want, such as other Psalms, or verses from Revelation) to help you think of motives for praising Him. Try not to *ask* God for anything during this time, but just express *praise* to Him.

13. YOUR SECRET WEAPON

Because of the secular influence in our society, we are accustomed to interpreting almost everything that happens to us from a material perspective, forgetting the *spiritual* dimension. For example, when we get sick, we tend to analyze the biological aspects: What virus do I have? How did I get it? What medicine should I take? These are all valid questions. However, there is also a spiritual dimension to everything. We are in spiritual warfare.

READ EPHESIANS 6:10-20.

According to verse 12, what are our real enemies?

Since the creation of the world, Satan has been trying to destroy humanity. Still, God is stronger, and He is always fighting against the influence of evil, causing all things to work out for our salvation.

If you are sick, you should use the physical means God has given you to treat your condition. For example, many times you need to see a doctor and take the medicine he prescribes. Nevertheless, don't forget that you should also pray, because the sickness is part of a spiritual battle.

Write down the parts of your spiritual armor, according to Ephesians 6:14-18:

Prayer is our *secret weapon* against the enemy, because our battle is spiritual. Prayer is our direct communication with the Lord, who directs all the heavenly armies against evil.

According to verse 18. ...

How should we pray?

When should we pray?

For whom should we pray?

There are good spirits and evil spirits. In human events, Satan and his demons are acting to do us harm, but at the same moment, God and His angels are acting for our good. If you break your arm, Satan desires it for evil, but the Lord will turn it into something good.

READ ROMANS 8:28-31.

In how many things does God work for good?

Why? What does God want to do in us? For what did He predestine us?

READ GENESIS 50:20.

Joseph's brothers had betrayed him. They had sold him as a slave to the Egyptians. But while in Egypt, he had risen to a high place in the government and was able to store wheat and help all his family when there was a famine.

How did Joseph interpret the fact that his brothers had betrayed him? What did he say?

In the same event, Satan meant evil, but God meant it for good.

What Satan especially wants is for us to sin. That's why prayer is so important, to ask the Lord to free us from the power of sin.

READ MATTHEW 6:13.

What should we pray, according to Jesus?

READ HEBREWS 4:14-16.

What does this passage teach us about Jesus?

That's why He can understand us and help us when we are tempted.

What should we do when we are tempted, according to verse 16?

READ 1 JOHN 4:4 AND 1 CORINTHIANS 10:13.

How do these verses encourage you in your spiritual struggle?

REVIEW

Why is prayer so important, according to this lesson?

FOR DISCUSSION

1. What would you say to a person who has prayed fervently for something and has not seen an answer to the prayer?

2. What would you say to a person who asks why we should pray if God already has everything planned?

EXERCISE

Think about some things that are concerning you. It might be family matters, personal matters, friends, church, work, health, finances, or social issues, for example. Spend time praying about these matters, considering how they are part of the larger scheme of spiritual warfare.

14. HOW CAN I SHARE MY FAITH WITH OTHERS?

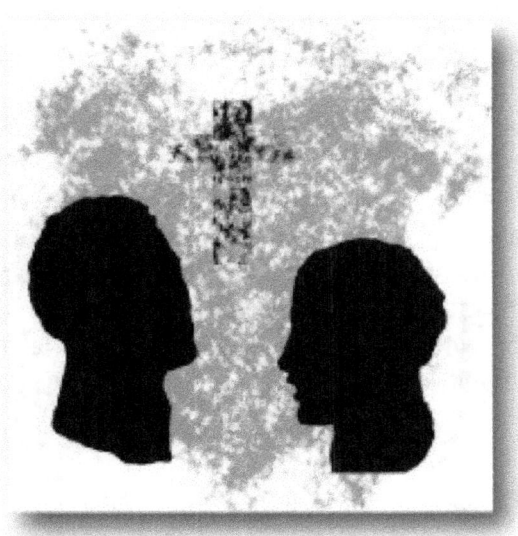

Suppose you were the only Christian in the world. If during one year one person came to know the Lord because you shared your faith with him or her, then the following year each one of you led another person to Christ, and you continued to double like this in numbers every year, how many years do you think it would take before everybody in the world became a Christian?

Two hundred years? One hundred? No....
Only thirty-three years!

This encourages you, doesn't it? It means that if we all ask the Lord to give us opportunities to share our faith and look for the ways He might be opening doors, the lives of many people can be transformed.

Maybe you would like to share your faith, but you need help learning how. This lesson gives you a simple outline of the gospel. It's a suggested guideline that will give you more confidence, but it's not meant to be mechanically repeated. All people are different, and we should adapt our message to make it clear to each person. The truth remains the same, but we can explain it in different ways. Furthermore, we can't convert anybody; only the Holy Spirit can do that. He works in peoples' hearts to lead them to their own personal relationship with Christ. The important thing is to develop a friendship and carry on a respectful dialogue regarding spiritual things.

READ 1 PETER 3:15

What does Peter tell us to do?

Read the contents of the following tract called *A New Harmony* and answer the review questions to help you learn it.

A NEW HARMONY

Have you ever asked yourself, "Why does the world seem so out of tune?" "Why are there so many problems?"

There is war, violence, sickness, hunger, poverty, injustice, fear, tragedy, racism, hatred, and death. Where do these problems come from? You may also ask, "What is the solution? How can we obtain a peaceful world?"

The Bible gives the explanation and the solution: There are three things you should *know* and three things you should *do* to help in the process of transforming the world into a new society of harmony and peace. The process starts with you!

THREE THINGS YOU SHOULD KNOW

1. CREATION
In the beginning God created everything in perfect harmony.

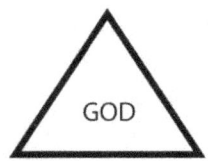

And God saw all He had made, and it was very good.
(Genesis 1:31)

2. CORRUPTION

Nevertheless, man disobeyed God, and as a result, the harmony turned into conflict. Adam represented all humanity, and he failed. Now all people are sinners, and we deserve eternal separation from God.

The relations were broken between:

> Man and God,
> Man and his neighbor,
> Man and nature, and
> Man and his own soul.

Therefore, just as sin entered the world through one man, and death through sin, and in this way death came to all men, because all sinned. (Romans 5:12)

3. CHRIST

This is why Jesus came into the world. He lived a perfect life, without sin. He died on the cross, suffering the punishment for sin in our place. He rose from the dead, winning the victory over sin, over Satan, and over death. Thus, Christ earned man's reconciliation with God and began to restore the relationships that were broken by sin, establishing His eternal kingdom.

For God was pleased to have all his fullness dwell in him, and through him to reconcile to himself all things, whether things on earth or things in heaven, by making peace though his blood, shed on the cross. (Colossians 1:19,20)

YOU can participate in the process of making a peaceful world and extending God's kingdom. First, you yourself should be reconciled to God, because your sin has also separated you from Him. Then you can help others experience the same peace.

THREE THINGS YOU SHOULD DO

1. RECEIVE

Receive forgiveness for your sins. God's pardon is free, because Jesus already took the punishment we deserved. You just need to sincerely ask for forgiveness. He takes away your sin and gives you the righteousness of Jesus. Doing this, you will be reconciled with Him, experience healing peace, and *spend eternal life in God's presence*.

You may not consider yourself such a bad person compared to others, but you must admit that you have done things that have offended God and brought conflict into the world. Besides, God looks at the heart and knows that our motives are not pure.

...There is no one righteous, not even one! (Romans 3:10)

For the wages of sin is death, but the gift of God is eternal life in Christ Jesus our Lord. (Romans 6:23)

If we confess our sins, he is faithful and just and will forgive us our sins and purify us from all unrighteousness.
(1 John 1:9)

Therefore since we have been justified through faith, we have peace with God through our Lord Jesus Christ. (Romans 5:1)

2. RELINQUISH

You need to relinquish the control of your life, turning it over to the Lord. Make the decision to become His disciple and follow Him. Trust Him to guide you and always do what is best for you. Then you will begin to experience a new life of joy, living more and more in harmony with others.

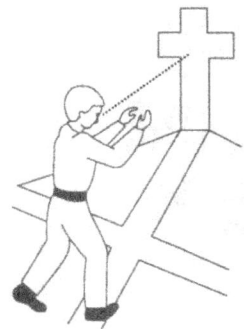

If we live, we live for the Lord, and if we die, we die for the Lord. So whether we live or die, we belong to the Lord. (Romans 14:8)

Submit yourselves, then, to God. (James 4:7)

You can take these two steps in the form of a prayer. God loves you and He will hear you. Ask forgiveness and turn your life over to Him.

3. REPEAT

Repeat this same message to others, so the process of reconciliation can be *repeated* in them. This way, the world can be transformed little by little, one person at a time, beginning from within people's hearts! This is the way God establishes His kingdom. It's the beginning of a *NEW HARMONY WHICH WILL LAST FOREVER!*

> *Therefore, go and make disciples of all nations....*
> (Matthew 28:19)

> *You are the salt of the earth.... You are the light of the world.*
> (Matthew 5:13,14)

REVIEW

Now you can learn to present the gospel, using the outline of the tract above.

First, write the introductory questions:

> *Why _____ ?*

> *What is the _____ ?*

The basic outline is simple:

> *There are three things you should _____.*

> *There are three things you should _____.*

There are three "C's" and three "R's":

Three things you should know:

        C _____

        C _____

        C _____

Three things you should do:

        R _____

        R _____

        R _____

Now learn to explain the points:

In the first two points, we explain where all problems come from. God didn't make the world that way, and He is not to blame. Man destroyed everything with sin.

In the third point, we explain the solution that God provided in Christ. This is the heart of the gospel. There are three aspects: His perfect life, His death on the cross, and His resurrection.

Now we need to relate these historical facts to the person with whom we are sharing the gospel. The person needs to see that the process of changing the world begins in his own heart and in his personal relationship with Jesus. He or she needs to accept Christ's forgiveness and turn his life over to Him. But it's important to emphasize that this is not only about individual salvation; it's much bigger. It's about establishing God's kingdom. That's why he should share the message with others.

Now you can ask the person what he or she thinks about it. Take time to talk about his relationship with God. Ask about his spiritual background. For example, did his family go to church? Does he? Has he ever read at least parts of the Bible? Does he believe in God? If he shows interest and understanding, you may ask if he wants to take the three steps of commitment: Receive, Relinquish, and Repeat. Don't pressure him. When he is ready for a commitment, you can help him say a prayer, but it should be in his own words. It may take days, weeks, months, or even years!

If he makes a decision, you can assure him that he has eternal life and that he will be an instrument of peace and harmony in the world.

Now, review the Bible verses so that you can quote them or learn to say them in your own words.

Genesis 1:31

Romans 5:12

Colossians 1:19, 20

Romans 3:10

Romans 6:23

1 John 1:9

Romans 5:1

Romans 14:8

James 4:7

Matthew 28:19

Matthew 5:13,14

EXERCISE

Practice a presentation of the gospel out loud with another friend. You might use the guideline from this lesson, or you might develop your own way to share the gospel. The important thing is to be "prepared to give an answer to everyone who asks you to give the reason for the hope that you have" (1 Peter 3:15).

15. HOW CAN I HELP CHANGE THE WORLD?

As mentioned in the presentation of the gospel in the previous lesson, when we give our lives over to the Lord, He begins to transform our hearts and we become *the salt of the earth* and *the light of the world*. We bring peace into the world and begin to transform the rest of society.

How does this process work? It starts with a loving attitude of *service*. In this lesson, we will look at this important aspect of the ministry of every believer.

READ JOHN 13:1-5.

What did Jesus want to show his disciples here?

READ MARK 9:33-35.

What were the disciples arguing about on the road?

How did Jesus answer their question?

READ MATTHEW 25:31-40.

Write down the different ways in which you can serve your neighbor, according to this passage:

What is the point of verse 40?

READ 1 JOHN 4:7-21.

If we don't love our brother, what does it reveal about us?

READ 1 JOHN 3:16-18.

What is the challenge for us in this passage?

READ JAMES 2:14-17.

How should true faith manifest itself?

God's love fills our hearts and flows out from us toward our neighbor. Faith is expressed in obedience. This has an impact on all of society. We are transformed as individuals, the church is also transformed, and the influence continues extending out into all areas of society.

READ MATTHEW 5:13-14.

Explain in your own words what you think these analogies mean.

READ MATTHEW 13:31-33.

Explain how you understand the first parable. What does it teach us about our influence in the world?

Explain how you understand the second parable. What does it teach us about our influence in the world?

These two parables suggest that the Kingdom of God grows and changes all of society. We could illustrate this with the figure of a cross that expands outward, representing the work of Christ in us and through us. First, the Lord changes the individual, then He changes His spiritual community, the church, then finally He changes the world, the rest of society, through us. The influence of the Kingdom is like the concentric circles formed when you throw a rock in a lake. As the church fulfills its integral ministry, the Lord's arms are extended into the world, manifesting His love. The church becomes a model for the world as a community of people being transformed into the image of Christ.

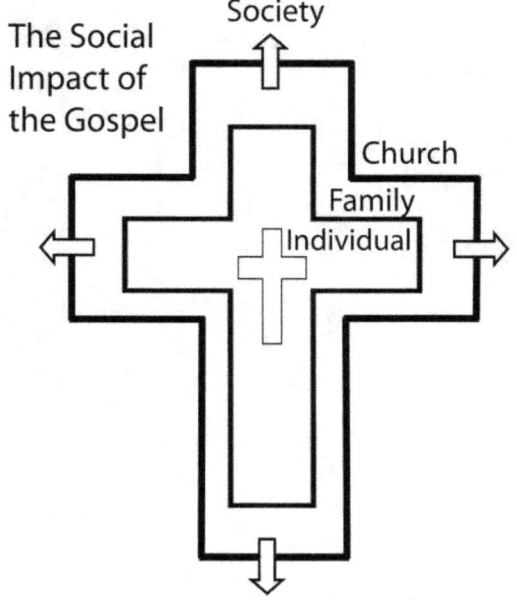

The Social
Impact of
the Gospel

Society

Church
Family
Individual

REVIEW

1. Who is the greatest in the Kingdom of God?

   He who S _____ the others.

2. We are the S _____ of the earth and the

   L _____ of the world.

3. True faith expresses itself in Good W_____.

4. When we serve a brother or sister, we are serving _____.

5. Draw the illustration of how the gospel makes an impact on all of society.

FOR DISCUSSION

Think of several concrete ways in which you and your local church can serve your neighbor and help change your community. Share your ideas.

16. HOW CAN I TEACH A BIBLE STUDY?

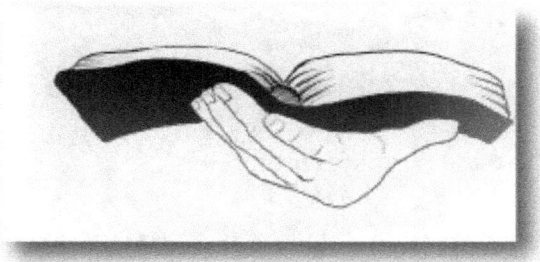

In a previous lesson, we studied how to do an analysis of a Bible passage, thinking especially about your own personal study. Now we're going to look at some guidelines for teaching others what you learn from your Bible study. First, we will look at some principles about Christian education.

READ EPHESIANS 4:11-13.

According to this passage, what is the purpose of education in the church? What do we want to accomplish?

This gives us a lot to think about! On the one hand, some people seem to teach only information and abstract doctrine, without practical application. On the other hand, some people tend to emphasize practical things, but don't use the Bible as a basis for their teaching, and it doesn't lead to real changes either. What we want is solid Bible teaching that leads to practical changes. Often people speak of the need to transform "head, hands and heart."

READ 2 TIMOTHY 3:16-17.

For what are the Scriptures useful?

READ LUKE 20:20-26.

How did Jesus use a question in this moment?

A good teacher does not only *teach*, but helps the students *learn*. A good way to help somebody learn is to ask questions. Sometimes a teacher thinks only about what he is saying, and not about what the students are learning. If he has good ideas, he thinks he is doing a good job. However, it is possible that they don't understand, or that they are not as interested in his ideas as he assumes. A good teacher knows how to put himself in the students' place and help them see clearly what he wants to get across. A good teacher helps the students participate. We retain little of what we *hear*, more of what we *experience* for ourselves, and even more of what we *discover* for ourselves. If you are leading a Bible study, let the others discover the truth for themselves in the Word, and let them talk. They will learn more if they are actively involved.

READ JOHN 15:1-7.

What illustration does Jesus use here?

A good teacher also uses illustrations. Jesus always talked of concrete things from daily life that everyone could understand.

There are many forms of teaching: a class at church, a Bible Study at home, preaching a sermon, or even informal conversation. We will give some suggestions for leading a home Bible Study and for teaching a class.

HOME BIBLE STUDY

You could use some Bible Study booklet with prepared lessons (such as this very book you are studying). But you can also prepare your own lesson. We recommend that you prepare the content of your study using the method of *Bible Analysis* that you learned in a previous lesson in this book. Then you can use the same three steps to ask questions to the group.

For example, you studied John 3:16 in the lesson on *Bible Analysis*. The following questions are examples of what you could use for a home study:

OBSERVATION
Ask the group:
> 1. Who are the people mentioned in the verse?
> 2. What are the verbs (action words)?
> 3. What did God do?
> 4. What motivated Him to do it?

INTERPRETATION
Ask:
> 1. Is there some word you don't understand?
> 2. Is there some phrase that is not clear?
> 3. Is there some concept that needs explanation?

Ask the people to look for answers within the same passage, or chapter, or within the same book of the Bible. If necessary, use a dictionary for words, or a concordance.

Other possible questions:
> 1. What does the word *world* mean here?
> 2. What does it mean that Jesus was the *only begotten* son?
> 3. In what way did God *give* His son?
> 4. What does it mean to *believe* in Jesus?
> 5. What does it mean to have *eternal life*?

APPLICATION
Ask:
> 1. What does this verse have to do with our lives?
> 2. Do you find in the verse:

        a. a promise?

        b. an example?

        c. a truth?

        d. a moral principle?

3. What changes should we make in our "head, hands, and heart" to make applications of this verse?

A CLASS

Again, you can prepare your own class, using what you learned from the *Bible Analysis* that you did of some passage. A class is different from a Home Bible Study because you may be more limited for time, and the number of people may make it hard for everyone to participate. You may have to talk more. We suggest the following plan for a one-hour class *with young people or adults*:

Prayer

Introduction

> The introduction should be something to get their attention and show the importance of what you are going to study. You may want to give an illustration or ask a question for reflection.

Bible Lesson

> This should be a summary of what you learned in your Bible Analysis. It should be brief, to the point, and practical. It's best to make one main point clear, rather than confusing them with many ideas. Explain

your point briefly, then use illustrations to make it clear.

Dialogue

Let them ask questions and make their own comments.

Conclusion

Draw conclusions and make practical applications.

Prayer

EXERCISE

Select a Bible text and prepare a Home Bible Study or a class for church, following the steps suggested above.

REVIEW

1. What is the purpose of education in the church?

2. The important thing is not so much what the teacher *teaches* but what the student _____.

3. It helps to use good I _____.

4. Good application seeks to transform H_____, H_____ and H_____.

17. HOW CAN WE ENCOURAGE ONE ANOTHER?

One of the greatest benefits of being a Christian is the fellowship we have with our brothers and sisters in Christ. We are members of one body, and each one needs the other, especially for encouragement. We will do a brief study in this lesson of how we can encourage one another and keep good relationships.

READ HEBREWS 10:24-25.

What should we encourage one another to do, according to this passage?

What should we not *stop* doing?

READ 2 CORINTHIANS 1:3-7.

According to this passage, how can we turn our sufferings into something positive?

READ EPHESIANS 4:15.

What are the two elements that work together to help us become more like Christ?

Neither one is sufficient by itself. To speak the truth without love can be cruel. To speak with supposed "love," but without the truth, is dishonest and hypocritical.

READ EPHESIANS 4:29.

What should our words do, according to this passage?

READ 1 CORINTHIANS 12:4-7.

For what purpose does the Spirit give us gifts?

READ 1 CORINTHIANS 12:21-26.

Why does every Christian need his brothers and sisters in Christ?

RESOLVING CONFLICTS

We should use our tongues to encourage one another and build each other up, but unfortunately sometimes this is not the case, and there are resulting conflicts between brethren. What should we do to resolve these problems? We're going to look at an important passage that helps us maintain good relationships within the church.

READ MATTHEW 18:15-17.

What is the first step to take when someone offends you?

According to this, is it correct to go to a third person to complain about what someone else did to you?

If the person who offended you does not listen to you, what is the second step?

137

If he still does not listen, what is the third step?

Note: This third step means that the authorities of the church take disciplinary measures with the offending person, taking away his privileges as a member. The purpose is to bring him back to the Lord.

READ MATTHEW 18:21-35.

If a brother who has offended us asks for forgiveness, then offends us again, how many times should we forgive him?

(This is a way of saying as many times as he asks for forgiveness.)

Tell the story of the king and the two servants in your own words.

Note: A denarius was worth one day of work for a common laborer. A talent of silver was worth about 6,000 times as much. So 10,000 talents would be about 60 million denarii. This would be an enormous amount, impossible for a normal person to pay in many lifetimes.

What happened to the first servant for not forgiving the second one?

What is the point that Jesus is making with this story?

To *forgive* means to decide not to make the other person pay for what he has done. That is, even though he has not repaired the damage he has caused (and sometimes it *can't* be repaired), you can treat the other person as if he had not hurt you. Maybe you can't completely forget what he has done, but you can decide not to punish him for it. You may even still feel bad about it, but you can leave the whole problem with the Lord and let Him take care of it.

In this lesson we have studied some basic principles about maintaining good relationships. If these guidelines are not followed, the whole church will suffer and may even be divided. If they are followed, you can avoid letting conflicts become serious.

REVIEW

1. We should use our tongues to E _____ others.

2. If someone offends us, we should follow the three steps for reconciliation:

a.

b.

c.

3. What does it mean to *forgive* someone?

FOR DISCUSSION

1. What do you think is the cause of most conflicts between people?

2. Have you learned something new about resolving conflicts? Explain what.

3. If someone has difficulty in forgiving an offense, what would you say to him?

18. WHAT ARE MY GIFTS?

Even though all believers should exercise all aspects of the integral ministry (worship, prayer, teaching, evangelism, service, and fellowship), each individual has special gifts that he can use to help the church grow. Just like a doctor has been prepared to confront all kinds of medical needs, but also has an area of specialization, the Holy Spirit equips you for many kinds of ministry, but He gives you a special area (or areas) where you can make a unique contribution. It is a wonderful blessing to discover your gifts so you can use them to their maximum potential.

READ 1 TIMOTHY 4:14 AND 2 TIMOTHY 1:6

What is Paul's charge to Timothy?

READ 1 CORINTHIANS 12:7-11.

Note the gifts mentioned in this passage.

READ 1 CORINTHIANS 12:27-31.

List the gifts mentioned in these verses:

READ 1 CORINTHIANS 13:1-3.

What is necessary for the gifts to be used properly?

READ ROMANS 12:6-8.

Name the gifts mentioned in this passage:

Do you think you have some of the gifts in the passages you have read? Which ones?

These lists of gifts are not meant to be complete. Maybe you can think of other gifts that are not mentioned in these passages. It should be something that the Lord uses to help others grow in Christ.

Write down your ideas:

Maybe you don't know exactly what your gifts are, but you think you can minister best in one or two of the six areas of the integral ministry. Try to put these areas in order. Put a "1" beside the area in which you feel strongest, a number "2" beside the second strongest, and so on.

_____ Worship

_____ Prayer

_____ Evangelism

_____ Service

_____ Teaching

_____ Fellowship

You may ask, "What is the difference between a *talent* and a *spiritual gift*?" A gift is used to build up the church, whereas a talent may not necessarily bring spiritual benefits. For example, if someone can sing well, but his or her singing does not bring spiritual blessings to others, it is simply a talent. (We could still call it a *gift* in a broader sense, or a *natural gift*, but not a *spiritual* gift.) However, a talent may *become* a spiritual gift if it is used for strengthening people in the church.

The church is one body with different members, united but diverse. If we work together, we can accomplish great things! Each one has his place, and nobody should look down on the gifts of others. On the contrary, we should encourage one another to use our gifts to help others.

REVIEW

1. For what should spiritual gifts be used?

2. Write down some of the spiritual gifts mentioned in 1 Corinthians 12 and Romans 12.

3. Explain in your own words the difference between a spiritual *gift* and a *talent*:

EXERCISE

After identifying what you think some of your gifts are, ask several friends from the church to tell you what gifts they see in you. If what they say coincides with what you thought, you were probably right. Wait to see if the Lord confirms your gifts, observing how He gives you opportunities to help others.

If you have been able to confirm some of your gifts, think of how you can use them to serve the Lord. Write down your ideas:

FOR DISCUSSION

1. If someone doesn't know what his spiritual gifts are, how would you help him discover them?

2. Why is it hard for some people to recognize their gifts?

3. What gifts are most common among the Christians you know? What gifts are least common?

19. HOW CAN I KNOW GOD'S WILL?

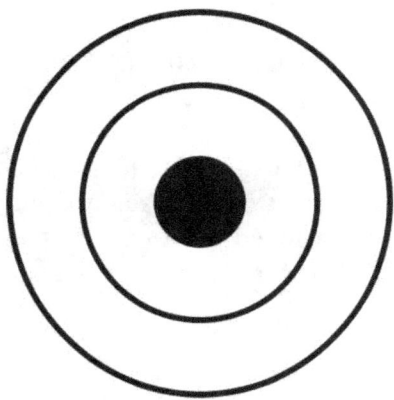

People sometimes become confused about the way God guides us to know His will. For example, if you are looking for a used car to buy and you see one with a Christian bumper sticker, that doesn't necessarily mean God is telling you it's the car you should buy. Just because the luxurious house next door goes on sale doesn't mean God is telling you that you should buy it, especially if it is beyond your means. If a young lady applies to several colleges, the first letter of acceptance she receives isn't necessarily a message from God telling her where she should study. We are going to examine a few principles for knowing God's will, to avoid making mistakes.

We could explain the principles with the illustration of concentric circles:

A. THE FIRST CIRCLE

READ 2 TIMOTHY 3:16-17 AND PSALM 119:9-11.

How does the Lord guide us, according to these passages?

The first circle is the most important one, because it draws the borderline between sin and obedience. Inside the circle is what God has commanded in His Word. If we follow these biblical norms of right and wrong, then we are doing what is correct.

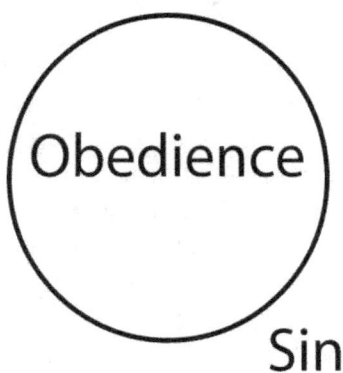

Therefore, to know God's will, the first step is to *study His Word.* You should obey the biblical norms first. Doing this, you will be within the first circle. For example, we don't have to wonder whether we should steal from the cash box at work or cheat on an exam in school, because the Bible forbids stealing and lying.

B. THE SECOND CIRCLE

However, while the Bible gives the guidelines we need, it doesn't tell us exactly what to do in every situation. For example, the Bible tells us we should help people in need, but it doesn't tell us exactly what people or exactly how we should help them. There are important questions, like which career to choose, what job to apply for, or where to live, that the Bible does not answer specifically. As a result, sometimes we are uncertain what God's will is.

READ PHILIPPIANS 1:9-11.

What should we learn to discern and approve?

READ 1 CORINTHIANS 6:12.

What distinction is made in this text?

READ JAMES 1:5.

What can we ask of God to help us make decisions?

As our loving heavenly Father, He helps us make the decision that is *best* for us. It may be the best alternative among several that are *permitted*. This is the second circle within the bigger one. In the first one, the Lord guides us (He commands us!) to do what agrees with His *biblical norms*. In the second one, He guides us to do the *wise* thing, the *excellent* thing. If we don't obey His *rules*, we are sinning. However, if we don't do what is *best*, we may not necessarily be sinning, but we are losing the benefits of using good judgment.

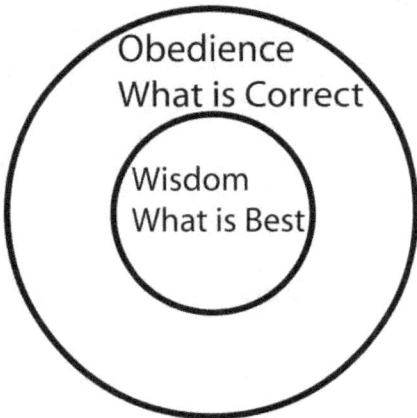

For example, it's good to help all kinds of people, but you don't want to give your donations to just any organization or just any person that asks for help. You want to be wise about it. Here you enter the second circle.

How does the Lord guide you in this area? We will look at four ways. Look up the passages and write down the different elements God uses:

READ JAMES 1:5.

What should we do to obtain wisdom?

READ PSALM 119:105.

What does God use to guide us?

When we talked about the first circle, we recommended using the Bible to look for God's ethical norms. Now you can read the Scriptures to find principles of *wisdom* as well. For example, the person you marry should be someone with good character, who can encourage you spiritually. You might read Proverbs, for example, to find passages regarding good character.

READ PROVERBS 11:14.

Write the third way God guides us to make a wise decision:

Ask for advice from friends and family, especially from mature Christians. They may realize whether the person you want to marry is a good person for you or not. They could be wrong, of course, but their opinion can help you decide.

READ PHILIPPIANS 1:9-11.

To discern what is best and be filled with righteousness, our love needs to abound in what?

Think about this: You need to *know* about the situation and the people involved to make a wise decision. For example, to help decide on a career, you need to consider your gifts and capacities and compare them with the requirements of the career. To decide where to live, you should think about factors such as your job, your family, where there is a good church, and where you can afford it. To decide on a church to attend, you should consider aspects such as whether the teaching is biblical and practical, whether the worship service is done "in Spirit and in truth," whether the fellowship is encouraging, and whether the activities of the church reflect a biblical perspective of Christian ministry. To make a wise decision, you need to examine the details surrounding the situation. You can't examine everything, of course, and you should avoid getting bogged down in details that are not important. Nevertheless, you need to take some time to think seriously about big decisions.

In summary, there are four ways the Lord leads you to a *wise* decision:

      a. Prayer,
      b. The Word,
      c. Advice from others, and
      d. Knowledge of the situation.

C. THE POINT

Finally, there may be several "correct" decisions within the first circle, and there may be more than one "wise" alternative within the second circle. That is, even though it may sound strange, the Lord sometimes leaves you with several choices that are all good. Suppose, for example, that you have a hard time deciding between two careers. You have prayed, you have studied the Scriptures, you have asked for counsel, and you have considered the details of the situation, but still you are left with two or three possibilities. In this case, you have freedom to choose one of these *according to your own preference*.

The same may be true in looking for a church to attend. There might be several churches that have sound biblical teaching, a good time of worship "in Spirit and in truth," and a good variety of effective ministries. There is nothing wrong with choosing one of those churches that is close to where you live, where you feel welcome, and where you personally enjoy the worship service. Sometimes there are several options that are equally pleasing to the Lord, and you are free to choose.

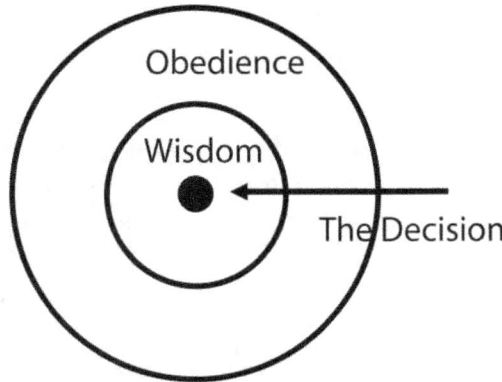

It's important to explain this, because sometimes people become paralyzed in the process of making a decision. They reach this stage in the process and can't go beyond it, because they are expecting the Lord to clearly show them the *point* in every decision. The Lord *may* guide you to the point, in fact He might show you in some special way. But that is not the way He *normally* guides us. In the majority of simple daily decisions, He simply leads us to the inner circle of wisdom, and if there are several possibilities, He lets us make the choice according to our own preference. He treats us like responsible adults. For example, you don't have to fret about which kind of toothpaste you buy. If there are several brands that are good for your health, and maybe even the same price, you can choose the one that you like best!

With this, we have not said everything about how the Lord guides us. The most important thing to remember is that the Lord never guides us to do anything against biblical principles of what is *correct* or biblical principles of what is *wise*, which are found in the Bible.

REVIEW

1. The Lord guides us in two senses:

a. He shows us moral principles to

 O _____ so we can do what is

 C _____.

b. He shows us what is W _____ so we can

 do what is B _____.

2. Write down four ways in which God guides you to make a *wise* decision (within the second circle):

 a.

 b.

 c.

 d.

3. Once we are obeying God's commands and using wisdom, the Lord often lets us decide among several valid alternatives, according to our own personal

 P _____.

FOR DISCUSSION:

1. What do you think of the explanation given in this lesson about how the Lord guides us? Do you agree? Is it helpful for you?

2. Share with the others about some difficult decision you have made, and how the Lord guided you.

3. Do you agree that sometimes the Lord does not show us clearly the *point*, but shows us different valid alternatives?

20. WHAT IS THE FULLNESS OF THE SPIRIT?

So that we can minister effectively to others, we need the Holy Spirit working in us and through us. Without considering all of the important teachings about the Holy Spirit and His work, this lesson gives some basic guidelines about what it means to experience the *fullness of the Holy Spirit*.

READ ROMANS 8:9 AND 1 CORINTHIANS 12:13.

According to these passages, do all believers have the Holy Spirit?

A person is renewed by the Holy Spirit in the moment of his conversion and receives the Holy Spirit in his heart for sanctification and guidance. If you belong to Christ, you have the Holy Spirit. However, not all believers are *full* of the Spirit. What does this phrase mean? Obviously, it doesn't mean that you can first have a part of the Spirit, and then later receive the rest of Him!

The *fullness* of the Holy Spirit can be understood in two senses: as a *characteristic* of a person, and as an *experience*. In Greek, the first use is expressed in the form of an adjective ("He is *full* of the Spirit."), and the second sense is expressed in the form of a verb in passive voice ("He was *filled* with the Spirit.")

Let's look at some examples:

A. AS A CHARACTERISTIC

READ ACTS 6:3.

What kind of people were they to choose as deacons?

READ ACTS 11:24.

How does this verse describe Barnabas?

In these two cases, to be full of the Spirit means spiritual maturity. These men showed the fruit of the Spirit (love, joy, peace, patience, kindness, goodness, faithfulness, gentleness and self-control, Galatians 5:22-23). Notice that this description was not something just for the moment, but it was a lasting characteristic.

In these cases, the word in Greek, *full*, is an adjective. Just as a person can be *kind*, *happy*, or *friendly*, for example, a person can also be *full of the Spirit*.

To sum up the first meaning of the *fullness of the Spirit*:

The term can be used as an adjective to describe a

    C _____ of a person.

It means he is spiritually

    M _____.

How can you be full of the Spirit in this sense? By using the means of growth that we have been studying in this book: the Word, prayer, the sacraments, and fellowship.

B. AS AN EXPERIENCE

The fullness of the Spirit can also refer to an *experience* in which the Lord *equips a person for a certain specific ministry*. In these cases, it would be more accurately translated as *filled with the Spirit*. (Unfortunately, some translations don't communicate this idea clearly.)

Read the following passages and identify what kind of ministry resulted from a person being filled with the Spirit:

EXODUS 31:1-3

Person:

Ministry:

MICAH 3:8

Person:

Ministry:

LUKE 1:67

Person:

Ministry:

ACTS 2:4

Person:

Ministry:

ACTS 4:31

Person:

Ministry:

ACTS 13:9-10

Person:

Ministry:

Notice that the same person can be filled repeatedly for different tasks. For example, Paul was filled with the Spirit in Acts 9:17 and again in Acts 13:9. Peter was filled several times (Acts 2:4, 4:8 and 4:31). This experience is for a specific occasion and is not a permanent characteristic.

To sum up the second sense of the *fullness of the Spirit*:

> The phrase can be used as a verb to describe

> an E _____.

> It means a person is equipped by the Holy

> Spirit for some special M _____.

What can you do to be filled with the Spirit in this sense?

READ LUKE 11:11-13.

The first thing you can do is *pray*. You can't control being filled with the Spirit. The Lord fills you with the Spirit for a special task when *He* wants to.

Secondly, you can put yourself in a position to receive this fullness by ministering to other people. As you begin to share your faith and help others grow, there may be moments when you need the special help of the Spirit and will sense His special blessing. For example, you may sense a burden to encourage someone or share the gospel with someone. You may suddenly have a clarity of thought and a capacity to explain something that you had never experienced before. You can sometimes tell that you were filled with the Spirit because of the results of what you have done. Maybe somebody was moved to believe in Jesus or maybe you were able to help somebody overcome a serious problem.

It's important to recognize that not everyone has the same experiences when they are filled with the Spirit. For example, not everyone speaks in tongues. Just as the Lord gives us different gifts, He also fills us with the Spirit for different purposes. The Bible teaches that the most important gifts are those that build up the Church, and that any ministry should be done in love.

READ 1 CORINTHIANS 12:27-13:1 and 14:1.

The following drawing summarizes the teachings of this lesson:

The Fullness of the Spirit

3. "FILLED" WITH THE SPIRIT:
A believer may have repeated
experiences of being prepared
for a special ministry.

2. "FULL" OF THE SPIRIT:
A believer grows spiritually,
showing the fruit of the Spirit,
becoming more like Christ.

1. INITIAL RECEIVING OF THE SPIRIT:
A person is renewed by the Holy Spirit
in the moment of his conversion, and
receives the Holy Spirit in his heart
for sanctification and guidance.

First, every believer receives the Holy Spirit when he becomes a Christian. This is represented by the figure of the white heart, which is now clean and forgiven. Then he or she begins a process of growth. The curved line represents this growth in fullness of the Spirit, that is, growth in maturity. The Xs represent the moments when the person is filled with the Holy Spirit for a specific ministry, which can happen at any time. The aspects of being "full" or "filled" do not always go together. A Christian could be immature and yet be filled with the Spirit for some special task. On the other hand, someone could be very mature and not have these experiences. However, normally a Christian experiences both kinds of fullness; as he grows in maturity, he also experiences special works of the Holy Spirit to help him minister to others.

REVIEW

1. Do all Christians have the Holy Spirit?

2. The phrase, *fullness of the Spirit,* can be understood in two senses. Identify the two meanings and explain them:

3. Make your own drawing of the diagram that shows the different meanings of the fullness of the Holy Spirit.

FOR DISCUSSION

1. Have you ever been filled with the Spirit for some special ministry? Talk about your experience.

2. Do you have any doubts about the Holy Spirit and His ministry? Explain them.

CONCLUSION

I hope the study of these lessons has been an encouragement to you in your process of spiritual growth! Please let me repeat that no human effort will produce real sanctification, unless we are trusting the Lord. Run the race with your eyes fixed on Jesus, the author and perfector of your faith!

> Human excellence,
> apart from God,
> is like the fabled flower which,
> according to the Rabbis,
> Eve plucked when passing out of Paradise.
> Severed from its native root,
> it is only the touching memorial of a lost Eden--
> sad while charming and beautiful,
> but dead. [1]
>
> Sir Charles Villiers Stanford

---

[1] Quoted by Steve Brown in *A Scandalous Freedom* (New York: Howard Books, 2004), p. 51.

Now I would like to ask a favor: Share what you have learned with others. Use your gifts and practice what you have learned about ministry. You could teach a Bible study using these same lessons or think of some other way to begin ministering to others, helping them press on and be transformed into the image of Christ. May the Lord guide you and bless you!

ANSWERS TO REVIEW QUESTIONS

The following are answers to the review questions at the end of each lesson:

Lesson 1

Sin no longer dominates you. (There is still a struggle with the old sinful nature, but sin no longer has control.)

Lesson 2

1. Your new purpose in life is to *glorify God*.
2. The goal of your spiritual growth is to *become like Jesus*.
3. Jesus manifests the *Fruit of the Spirit*.
4. Jesus manifests perfect *love*.
5. Your job description is to live your life like Jesus.

Lesson 3

1. You shall have no other gods.
2. You shall make no images or bow down to them.
3. You shall not misuse the name of God.
4. Keep the Sabbath day holy.

Lesson 4

1. You shall have no other gods.
2. You shall make no images or bow down to them.
3. You shall not misuse the name of God.
4. Keep the Sabbath day holy.
5. You shall honor your father and mother.
6. You shall not kill.
7. You shall not commit adultery.

8. You shall not steal.
9. You shall not lie.
10. You shall not covet.

Lesson 5

1. The secret for significant change in your life is to *keep your eyes on Jesus*.
2. Our righteousness comes from God, by *faith* from first to last.
3. The four Means of Grace are:
       a. The Word
       b. Prayer
       c. The Sacraments
       d. fellowship.

Lesson 6

Steps for Bible Analysis:
       I. Observation
       II. Interpretation
              A. Ask Questions
              B. Look for Answers
                     1. In the Bible
                     2. In Other Study Aids
       III. Application
              A. Promises
              B. Truths
              C. Ethical Principles
              D. Examples

Lesson 7

1. To ask for something in Jesus' name means to ask for it *to please Him*. (That is, with the motive of seeing His will done and with the attitude of seeking His honor.)
2. We can study the Bible to see if it is according to His will.
3. He may not grant our request because it is not the best thing for us. (Maybe He has something better for us, or maybe it is not the right time.)

Lesson 8

1. A sacrament is a ceremony instituted by Jesus to teach spiritual truths by means of material symbols.
2. Baptism symbolizes cleansing from sin, new life in Christ, and receiving the Holy Spirit. It is used especially to publicly receive believers and their children into the Church.
3. *Circumcision* is replaced by baptism.
4. The Lord's Supper symbolizes Christ's death for our sins, the unity of all believers, our dependence on the Lord, and the future banquet we will celebrate with Him. It is used especially to remember Jesus' death for us.
5. The *Passover* is replaced by the Lord's Supper.

Lesson 9

1. Fellowship
2. Love
3. According to Hebrews 10:25, we should stir up one another to love and good works, not neglecting to meet together, but encouraging one another.
4. A body

Lesson 10

The two basic steps for a Quiet Time are praying and reading the Bible. It's good to keep a notebook for writing down what you learn.

Lesson 11

THE MINISTRY

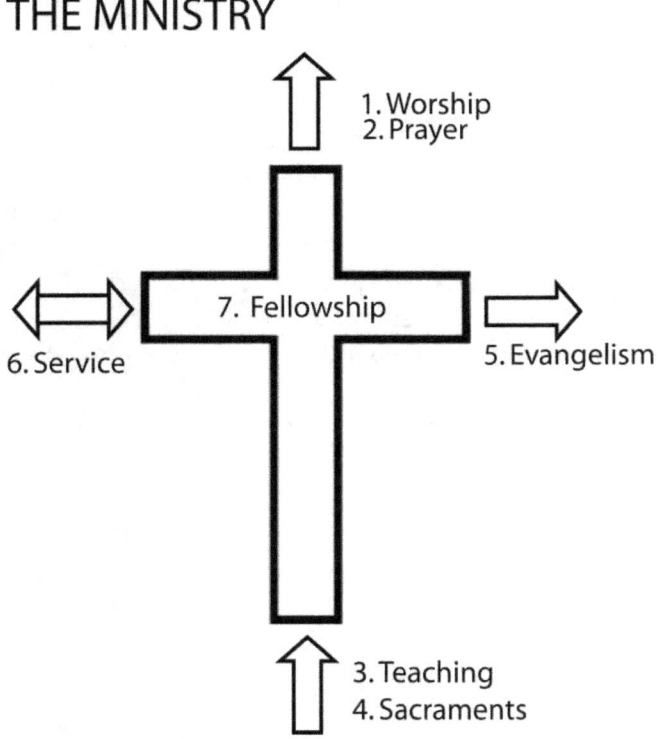

1. Worship
2. Prayer

7. Fellowship

6. Service

5. Evangelism

3. Teaching
4. Sacraments

Lesson 12

1. The most important reason to go to church is *to worship God*.
2. To worship literally means to *fall down before someone and kiss his feet*.
3. To worship in spirit and in truth means to worship with your heart, sincerely, and with your mind, using true concepts.

Lesson 13

Prayer is important because it is our secret weapon in our spiritual battle.

Lesson 14

The basic outline of the gospel presentation:

> Three things you should know:
> > The Creation
> > The Corruption
> > Christ
>
> Three things you should do:
> > Receive forgiveness
> > Relinquish the control of your life
> > Repeat the message to others

Lesson 15

1. *The one who serves* is the greatest in the kingdom of God.
2. We are the *salt* of the earth and the *light* of the world.
3. True faith expresses itself in *good works*.

4. When we serve a brother, we are serving *Christ*.

5.

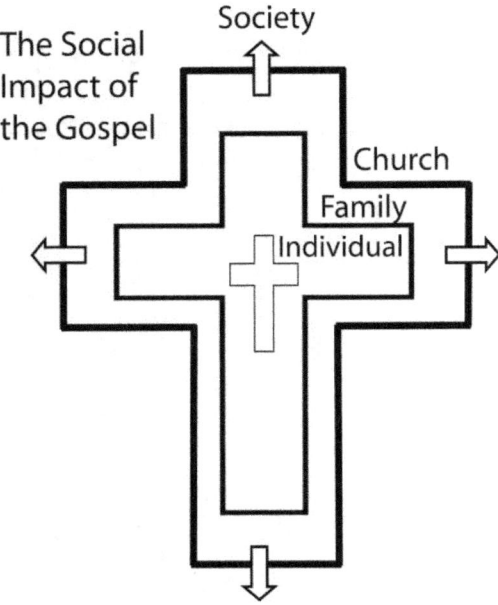

Lesson 16

1. The purpose of education in the church is to help the church and all its members become like Jesus.
2. The important thing is what the student *learns*.
3. It helps to use good *illustrations*.
4. Good application seeks to transform "head, hands, and heart."

Lesson 17

1. We should use our tongues to *encourage* others.

2. The three steps for reconciliation:

    a. Talk to the person who offended you.

    b. If he doesn't listen, go with one or two witnesses.

    c. If he still doesn't listen, tell the authorities of the church.

3. To forgive means to *decide not to make the other person pay for what he has done*.

Lesson 18

1. The gifts should be used to *help the church grow*.

2. 1 Cor. 12: wisdom, knowledge, faith, healing, miracles, prophecy, distinguishing spirits, tongues, interpreting tongues. Rom. 12: service, teaching, exhortation, giving, leading, mercy.

3. A *talent* does not necessarily bring spiritual blessings and help the church grow, but a *gift* does.

Lesson 19

1. The Lord guides us in two senses:

        a. He shows us moral principles to *obey* so we can do what is *correct*.

        b. He shows us what is *wise* so we can do what is *best*.

2. Four ways in which God guides us to make a wise decision:

        a. Prayer

        b. The Word

        c. Advice from others, and

        d. Knowledge of the situation

3. Preference.

Lesson 20

1. Yes, all Christians have the Holy Spirit.
2. Fullness of the Spirit can mean:
   a. a characteristic, indicating spiritual maturity ("full" of the Spirit), or
   b. an experience, being equipped for a special ministry ("filled" with the Spirit).

The Fullness of the Spirit

3. "FILLED" WITH THE SPIRIT:
A believer may have repeated experiences of being prepared for a special ministry.

2. "FULL" OF THE SPIRIT:
A believer grows spiritually, showing the fruit of the Spirit, becoming more like Christ.

1. INITIAL RECEIVING OF THE SPIRIT:
A person is renewed by the Holy Spirit in the moment of his conversion, and receives the Holy Spirit in his heart for sanctification and guidance.

www.ingramcontent.com/pod-product-compliance
Lightning Source LLC
Chambersburg PA
CBHW060424130626
46555CB00005B/2207